I Want to Be a Princess

Dawn McMillan

AF605216

I want to be a princess.
How can I be a princess?

If my dad was a king,
I would be a princess.

If my mum was a queen,
I would be a princess.

Here is a princess.
Her mum is a queen.

Princess Martha-Louise

I want to be a princess.
How can I be a princess?

If I married a prince,
I would be a princess.

She is a princess.
She married a prince.

Dad took me to a film
about a princess.
This princess
is called Fiona.

Dad and I looked at
a book about a princess.
This princess
is called Rapunzel.

Mum and I saw a film about a princess.

Mum and I looked at a book about a princess.

There are princess stories from all over the world.

Princess Maya is from India.

Princess Kwan-yin is from China.

Princess Diana

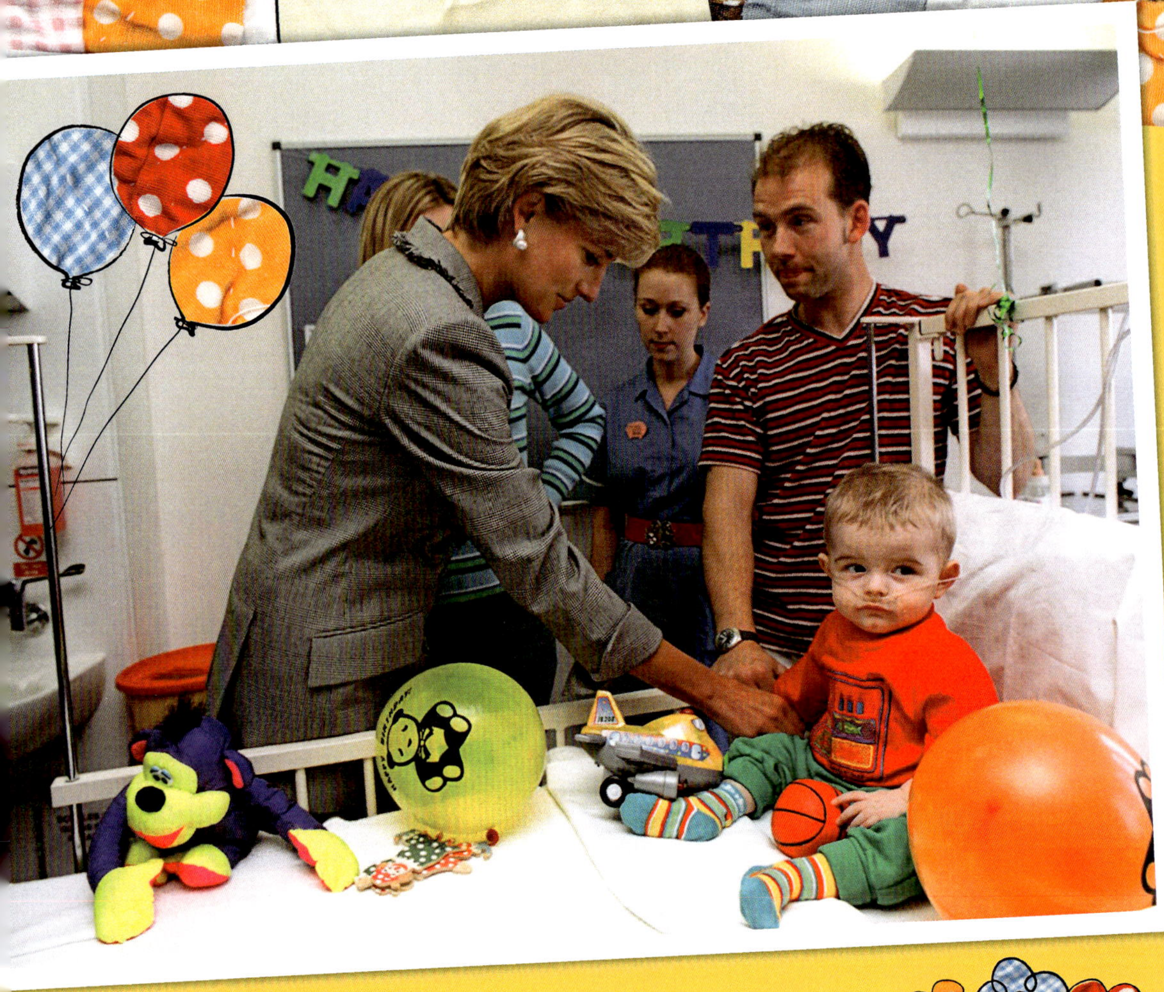

Princesses do lots of things.
They visit hospitals.

They visit schools.
They meet children.

I can be a princess.
I will dress up
like a princess.

I will wear
a crown.

Here I am.
I am a princess!